THE 13 ORIGINAL COLONIES

by Campbell Collison

BEARPORT
PUBLISHING

Minneapolis, Minnesota

Credits:

© Cover, clockwise from bottom left, Sidney E. King, artist/U.S. National Park Service/Public Domain; Tsekhmister/Shutterstock; RCPPHO-TO/Shutterstock; Title Page, 4, 5, 7, 9, 10, 13 top, 17 top, 21 top, 23 top, 25 bottom, Sidney E. King, artist/U.S. National Park Service/Public Domain; 4 right, John Gadsby Chapman (photograph courtesy Architect of the Capitol)/Public Domain; 5 top, Henry Brueckner/Public Domain; 6, 12, 14, 16, Joshua Avramson; 7 middle, Johann Zoffany/Public Domain; 8 top, Richard Josey after a picture by Alfred Walter Bayes/Public Domain; 8 bottom, Roman Samborskyi/Shutterstock; 9 top, William Halsall/Public Domain; 9 middle, The German Kali Works/Public Domain; 9 right,14, Jean Leon Gerome Ferris/Public Domain; 10 top, Public Domain; 11 top, Jean Leon Gerome Ferris/Public Domain; 11 middle, Sandra van der Steen/Shutterstock; 11 bottom left, LightField Studios/Shutterstock;11 bottom middle, Iakov Filimonov/Shutterstock; 11 bottom right, Pate, William, engraver/Public Domain; 12 right Dragon Images/Shutterstock; 13 middle, Swampyank/Creative Commons; 13 bottom, W. Endicott & Co./Library of Congress/Public Domain; 13 bottom middle, Elena Nichizhenova/Shutterstock; 13 bottom right, Public Domain; 15 bottom, Peter Lely/Public Domain; 16, Augusto Ferrer-Dalmau Nieto/Creative Commons; 17 middle, Tatiana Liubimova/Shutterstock; 17, ommaphat chotirat/Shutterstock; 17 bottom right, Bill Chizek/Shutterstock.com; 18 top, 19 top, 19 bottom, Everett Historical/Shutterstock; 18, Howard Pyle/Public Domain; 18 top right, suthas ongsiri/Shutterstock; 20 top, Edwin Austin Abbey/Public Domain; 20 left, Bob Pool/Shutterstock.com; 20, Ritu Manoj Jethani/Shutterstock.com; 21 middle left, Public Domain; 21 bottom left, Charles Andres/Public Domain; 21 middle right, Scipio Moorhead/Public Domain; 21 bottom left, Charles Andres/Public Domain; 21 bottom right, Benjamin Wilson/Public Domain; 22, T. J. Choleva (Eric Isselee/Shutterstock, Anthonycz/Shutterstock, Americanspirit/Dreamstime); 23 middle, Cookie Studio/Shutterstock; 23 right, Lucy/Shutterstock.com; 23 bottom, Gerard ter Borch/Public Domain; 24 top right, Eliza Susan Quincy/Public Domain; 24 middle, Magnus Binnerstam/Shutterstock; 24 bottom, 25 top, U.S. National Park Service/Keith Rocco, artist/Public domain; 25 middle, J Paulson/Shutterstock; 25 left, NTL Photography/Shutterstock.com; 25 bottom middle, Scott K Baker/Shutterstock.com; 25 bottom left, NTL Photography/Shutterstock.com; 25 bottom middle, Scott K Baker/Shutterstock.com; 26, ESB Essentials/Shutterstock.com; 27 top, John Trumbull/Public Domain; 27 middle, New Africa/Shutterstock; 27, Gelpi/Shutterstock; 29 bottom left, vitals/Shutterstock; 28-29, Austen Photography

Developed and produced for Bearport Publishing by BlueAppleWorks Inc.
Managing Editor for BlueAppleWorks: Melissa McClellan
Art Director: T.J. Choleva
Photo Research: Jane Reid
Editor: Marcia Abramson

Library of Congress Cataloging-in-Publication Data

Names: Collison, Campbell, author.
Title: The 13 original colonies / by Campbell Collison.
Other titles: Thirteen original colonies
Description: Minneapolis, Minnesota : Bearport Publishing Company, [2021] |
   Series: Xtreme facts: U.S. history | Includes bibliographical references
   and index.
Identifiers: LCCN 2020012959 (print) | LCCN 2020012960 (ebook) | ISBN
   9781647471248 (library binding) | ISBN 9781647471316 (paperback) | ISBN
   9781647471385 (ebook)
Subjects: LCSH: United States—History—Colonial period, ca.
   1600-1775—Juvenile literature. | United States—Social life and
   customs—To 1775—Juvenile literature.
Classification: LCC E188 .C694 2021 (print) | LCC E188 (ebook) | DDC
   973.2—dc23
LC record available at https://lccn.loc.gov/2020012959
LC ebook record available at https://lccn.loc.gov/2020012960

For more information, write to Bearport Publishing, 5357 Penn Avenue South, Minneapolis, MN 55419.
Printed in the United States of America.

Contents

Struggles at Jamestown

It was late 1609, and Jamestown **Colony** in Virginia was about to collapse. The water was making settlers sick. The harsh winter was starving them. They were eating their pets and even their shoe leather. And local Algonquian tribes were threatening to attack. The colonists were preparing to quit and go back to England when, in the spring of 1610, more English ships arrived with supplies and additional settlers. Jamestown was saved!

Jamestown was the first British colony to succeed in what became the United States.

YOU ARE A GENIUS, MR. ROLFE!

I'M GLAD THE TOBACCO PLANTS ARE HELPING.

Settler John Rolfe introduced a new and profitable crop for the colonists to grow—tobacco.

In 1614, **John Rolfe married Pocahontas**, a member of the Powhatan Nation. This created some peace between Jamestown and its Native American neighbors.

Pocahontas was a nickname that may have meant "playful one." Her given name may have been Matoax.

Pocahontas died during a trip to England in 1617. Soon, the peace between Jamestown and the Powhatan Nation fell apart.

Jamestown was not the first attempted colony. In 1587, English colonists had settled on Roanoke Island off the North Carolina coast. Roanoke would become known as the Lost Colony, after its settlers were never heard from again.

YEAH, I DON'T TRUST THOSE NEWCOMERS ANYMORE!

HAVE YOU HEARD? OUR POCAHONTAS IS DEAD.

The 13 Colonies

The first Europeans to settle in North America came for a number of reasons. Some were seeking wealth or treasure. Others were trying to claim more land for their home countries. And some were hoping to build a new life where they would be free to practice their religion. Over time, 13 colonies were established along the east coast of what would become the United States.

The 13 original colonies are divided into three groups: The New England colonies, the middle colonies, and the southern colonies.

A colony is an area of land that has been settled by people from another country and is ruled by that country.

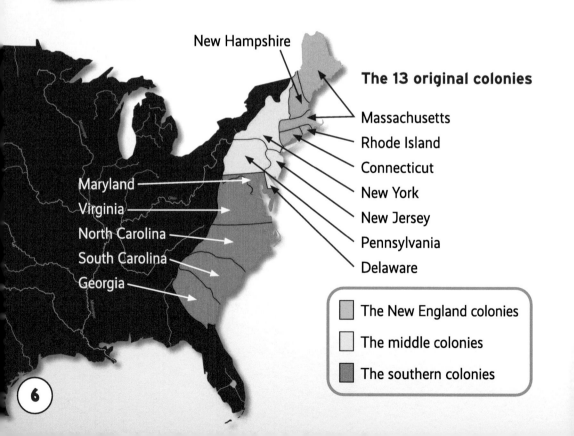

New Hampshire

The 13 original colonies

Massachusetts
Rhode Island
Connecticut
New York
New Jersey
Pennsylvania
Delaware

Maryland
Virginia
North Carolina
South Carolina
Georgia

The New England colonies
The middle colonies
The southern colonies

Jamestown had only 100 settlers in 1607. By 1775, there were 2.5 million Europeans living in the 13 colonies.

I QUIT!

Before the American **Revolution**, England's King George III ruled the colonies. He was so upset at losing the war that he almost gave up the throne!

The first Europeans to arrive in North America found a long-established network of Native American tribal nations and settlements.

LOOK AT ALL THE PEOPLE HERE! WHERE DID THEY COME FROM?

THEY COULD ASK THE SAME QUESTION, YOU KNOW.

Plymouth and the Pilgrims

The *Mayflower* set sail from England in 1620 with about 100 passengers, nearly 30 crew members, and 2 dogs. Many of the settlers onboard were seeking religious freedom. The ship was headed for what was then northern Virginia, but stormy seas drove the ship off course. It ended up anchoring off the coast of present-day Massachusetts. The colonists selected a spot on the shores of Cape Cod Bay to settle, which became the Plymouth Colony. These men and women became known as Pilgrims.

It took more than two months for the *Mayflower* to cross the Atlantic Ocean.

The *Mayflower* was just 80 feet (24 m) long, about the length of 2 school buses.

The year 2020 marked the 400th anniversary of the *Mayflower's* voyage.

Tisquantum, or **Squanto**, was a member of the Patuxet tribe who understood English. He became a guide and translator for the Plymouth colonists.

Squanto had learned English after being kidnapped by an English explorer years before.

Native Americans and Colonists

In both Jamestown and Plymouth, relations between Native Americans and colonists were often strained by fear and distrust. Yet the early colonies would probably not have survived without the help and advice offered by Native Americans. Some colonial leaders tried to create **alliances** and trade agreements with neighboring tribes. More often than not, though, Native Americans were pushed off their tribal lands by bad or dishonest deals or all-out violence.

Samoset, an Abenaki leader, was the first Native American to greet the Plymouth colonists.

Trading goods for food helped the settlers survive.

What many people call the first Thanksgiving in 1621 was a three-day party. It was as much a **diplomatic** gathering as it was a harvest festival.

There may have been twice as many Native Americans as English colonists at the Thanksgiving celebration.

Much of the first Thanksgiving meal was probably deer and **shellfish**.

President **Abraham Lincoln** declared Thanksgiving an official holiday in 1863.

ARE YOU EXCITED FOR THE THANKSGIVING TURKEY?

MOM, I WANT SHELLFISH AND DEER MEAT FOR THIS THANKSGIVING!

LISTEN TO YOUR MOTHER, KID!

Spreading Out

English ships carrying more colonists arrived, and Plymouth Colony grew. Starting in 1628, the Massachusetts Bay Colony began settling much of what would become Massachusetts and northern New England. Colonists spread out and created farms and settlements as far north as what would become northern Maine. Some colonists sought land farther away in order to escape the strict religion of the Puritans that dominated the Plymouth and Massachusetts Bay colonies.

Rhode Island can brag about having the longest colony name—Rhode Island and Providence **Plantations.** That's still the state's official name!

Rhode Island isn't truly an island, but it does include more than 30 islands!

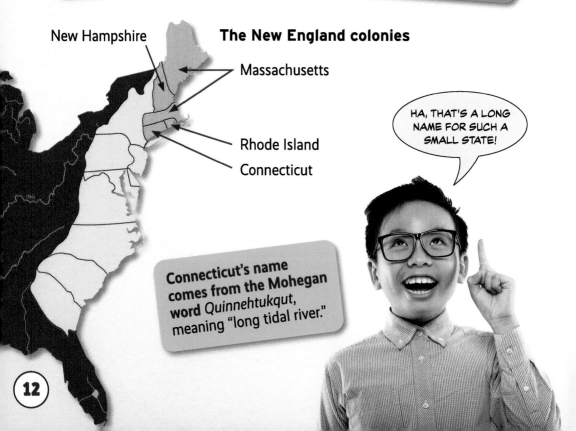

New Hampshire

The New England colonies

Massachusetts

Rhode Island

Connecticut

HA, THAT'S A LONG NAME FOR SUCH A SMALL STATE!

Connecticut's name comes from the Mohegan word *Quinnehtukqut,* meaning "long tidal river."

Even after settling in the Americas, some colonists grew restless. Looking for better land or more freedom, they found new areas to settle such as Vermont.

Touro Synagogue in Newport, Rhode Island, was founded in 1658. Today, it is the oldest synagogue building in the Americas.

Williams founded the First Baptist Church of Providence, but Rhode Island colonists were free to practice the religion of their choice.

Roger Williams was banished from Massachusetts by the Puritans. He left and founded the Rhode Island colony in 1636.

Providence was a busy port for the colonies and later became Rhode Island's capital.

The Middle Colonies

The English were not the first to settle the territory of the middle colonies. Dutch and Swedish trading companies began the colonies in what became Maryland, Delaware, Pennsylvania, New Jersey, and New York. After a series of wars, England took over these settlements. To colonists, it hardly mattered who controlled the territory. They were mainly interested in the rich farmland, fish-filled rivers, easy shipping, and religious freedom.

Pennsylvania

New York

New Jersey

Delaware

Pennsylvania was founded by William Penn, a **Quaker**, who promised religious freedom for all.

William Penn formed peaceful, respectful relationships with the Native Americans who lived in Pennsylvania.

Penn landed in 1682 and named the colony Pennsylvania.

New York City was originally New Amsterdam, part of the Dutch colony of New Netherland. In 1664, the Dutch surrendered it to England.

JUST LET THE ENGLISH TAKE OVER. THEY SEEM VERY POLITE!

Citizens of New Amsterdam did not want war, especially after hearing England would let them keep their land and their religious freedom. They begged the Dutch governor to surrender.

The middle colonies were referred to as the breadbasket because of all the wheat grown there.

The colony of New Jersey was named after the Isle of Jersey in the English Channel.

New York was named after the Duke of York, James Stuart, who was the brother of England's King Charles II.

JAMES, I DREAMT THAT ONE DAY A COLONY IN AMERICA WILL BE NAMED AFTER YOU.

I LIKE THE SOUND OF THAT, CHUCK!

The Southern Colonies

The southern colonies of Maryland, Virginia, Georgia, and the Carolinas grew quickly once colonists began migrating from England in large groups. The warm climate was ideal for growing **cash crops** such as corn, rice, and tobacco, which could be sold to the northern colonies or Europe. Yet the warm and often swampy land was also a breeding ground for disease.

The colony of Georgia was created to be a **buffer** between the Carolinas and Spanish settlements in Florida.

Maryland

Virginia

North Carolina

South Carolina

Georgia

Spanish Florida

HOW DO WE GET TO CAROLINA, DON DIEGO?

I DON'T THINK WE CAN, CABALLERO. LOOK, GEORGIA IS IN OUR WAY!

**Cash crops were sent to Europe on sailing ships.
Many planters became rich from their profits.**

Rice was an important southern crop because it could grow in swamps and marshes.

Maryland was a safe home for Roman Catholics, who were not treated fairly in the other colonies. One of the colony's founders, Lord Baltimore, was Catholic.

It took many workers to plant, pick, and pound the hulls off rice.

GUESS WHAT WE'LL BE HAVING FOR DINNER.

HMM . . .

LOOK AT ALL OF THESE RICE FIELDS!

Slavery in the Colonies

Much of the wealth of the American colonies was made possible by slave labor. Slave labor was used in the north until the first decade of the 1800s. Southern plantation owners first used European **indentured servants** as inexpensive field laborers. As their farms grew larger and spread westward, however, they began to rely on enslaved people from Africa. Meanwhile, northern merchants grew rich through the slave trade—the buying and selling of human beings.

Spanish **conquistadores** were the first to bring enslaved Africans to North America in 1565.

Sailors traded enslaved people for food at Jamestown in 1619. That exchange is often considered the start of the colonial slave trade.

Horribly, enslaved people were often sold and bought at large markets.

Tobacco became a huge cash crop in Virginia. In 1688 alone, more than 18 million pounds were grown there.

Enslaved workers did backbreaking work in brutal heat from dawn to dusk.

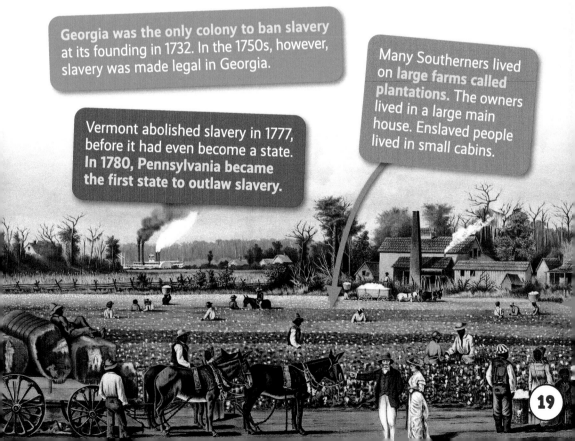

Georgia was the only colony to ban slavery at its founding in 1732. In the 1750s, however, slavery was made legal in Georgia.

Many Southerners lived on **large farms called plantations.** The owners lived in a large main house. Enslaved people lived in small cabins.

Vermont abolished slavery in 1777, before it had even become a state. In 1780, Pennsylvania became the first state to outlaw slavery.

Life on a Farm

Most early colonial settlers lived on farms. In the early years, colonists learned a lot about planting from local Native Americans. Farmers rode in horse-drawn carts to sell crops in nearby towns and markets. They used their profits to buy supplies, including cloth for making clothing, salt for cooking and preserving food, and tools for working.

In 1790, 9 out of 10 Americans lived on farms. Today, only 1 in 100 Americans lives on a farm or ranch.

Colonists learned to grow corn from Native Americans. Scots-Irish settlers even started raising hogs on corn rather than nuts and acorns as they had done in Europe.

Colonial kids worked with their parents as early as age seven. Younger kids did easy tasks like feeding chickens.

Colonial farming families worked from sunrise to sunset.

To get clean, people just washed their hands and faces. They took baths only a few times a year.

North America's first dairy cows were brought to Plymouth in the 1620s.

Towns and Villages

In the early days of a colony's founding, settlers lived close together for safety and protection. Even after people began spreading out to surrounding lands to create farms, villages and towns remained important. They became places to trade goods. **Meetinghouses** and churches were important town centers. Inns and taverns served travelers and sailors. Merchants and craftspeople began to thrive as town and village populations grew.

The first college in America was founded in 1636 in Boston, Massachusetts. Three years later, it was named after minister John Harvard, who gave the school money and books.

In early colonial villages, animals roamed freely. Hogs often wandered the streets.

Men met to relax, read newspapers, and discuss business and politics in taverns and coffeehouses.

The town's market was a place for farmers and merchants to sell their goods.

Wealthy professional men bought expensive powdered wigs made of yak and goat hair.

Most towns had a millinery shop that sold hats, aprons, cloth, and dressmaking materials.

YES, SIR! YOU CERTAINLY COULD USE ONE. YOUR OWN HAIR IS A **DISGRACE!**

WHERE CAN I BUY A WIG? DOWN THE STREET?

Women's Roles

Colonial women shared the labor of planting and harvesting on farms and managing shops and taverns in towns. In addition, they often cared for children, cooked meals, cleaned the clothes and house, and kept a garden. Despite all this work, women could not vote. Often, they could not own or sell property. Very few of them received any formal education. Even so, some women rose to positions of power.

Anne Hutchinson was kicked out of Massachusetts Bay Colony for her strong religious views and leadership of female Bible study groups.

One job open to colonial women was that of becoming a midwife—helping women deliver babies.

GREAT NEWS, SALLY! I'VE JUST DELIVERED YOUR SISTER'S BABY. LET'S HAVE TEA, AND I'LL TELL YOU ALL ABOUT IT.

WHO HAS TIME FOR TEA? THERE IS SO MUCH WORK TO BE DONE!

Even at night, colonial women worked by the glow of firelight. They would sew and mend clothes, wind wool, and knit.

Girls learned household skills and cared for younger children at an early age.

Anne Bradstreet is known as America's first female poet.

In 1773, Phillis Wheatley became the first African American woman to have a book of poems published. She was freed from slavery shortly thereafter.

YOU'RE MAKING SOME SERIOUS COIN, DEB!

Benjamin Franklin's wife, Deborah, managed a general store, a stationery shop, and many other businesses in Philadelphia.

AND YOU'LL KEEP YOUR HANDS OFF IT, BEN!

Moving Toward Independence

Despite hardships, the British colonies were taking root and becoming successful. Britain, however, was in debt and wanted to tax the colonies to raise money. The colonists were not pleased about the new taxes. Rebel groups began to rise up and protest. More British troops were sent to America to enforce the taxes and control the colonists. It wasn't long before anger and rebellion led to all-out war!

The Stamp Act of 1765 was a tax on every piece of printed paper, including newspapers and playing cards!

The Stamp Act was canceled after only a year, but a tax on tea soon followed.

I AM FED UP WITH YOUR TAXES! IT IS TIME TO GET RID OF YOUR BRITISH GREED!

DON'T WORRY, DEAR. THE CONGRESS WILL TAKE CARE OF IT!

YOU WILL PAY THE NEW TAX ON TEA, LIKE IT OR NOT!

In 1776, the **Second Continental Congress** announced the colonies' break from Britain with the **Declaration of Independence.**

John Hancock was president of the congress

John Hancock was the first to sign the Declaration of Independence—in BIG letters.

The first fighting of the American Revolution broke out on April 19, 1775, at the Battle of Lexington and Concord in Massachusetts.

One of the first student protests in American history, called the Butter Rebellion, was at Harvard University in 1755. Students, sick and tired of being served spoiled butter, led loud and violent protests.

APOLOGIES FOR MY SMELL!

U-S-A! U-S-A!

The 13 stripes on the American flag represent the 13 original colonies.

A Corny Doll
CRAFT PROJECT

Children in colonial times were very busy. They helped in the house and in the farmyard. Almost everything they used had to be made by hand, including candles, butter, cloth, and toys.

Children would use corncobs, wood, apples, walnuts, and gourds to make their own toys. Native Americans taught colonial settlers how to make corn husk doll toys.

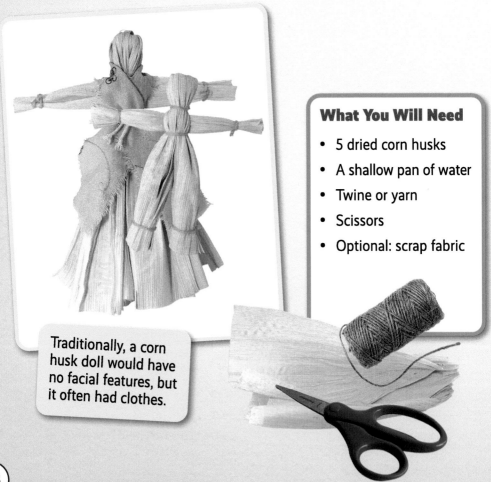

What You Will Need

- 5 dried corn husks
- A shallow pan of water
- Twine or yarn
- Scissors
- Optional: scrap fabric

Traditionally, a corn husk doll would have no facial features, but it often had clothes.

Step One

Soften the dried husks in a shallow pan of water for about 15 minutes. Take four husks and twist them around one another in clockwise fashion. Tie them together tightly with the twine about ½ inch (1.3 cm) from the end.

Tie

Step Two

Pull the husks back and over the tied end. Tie a string about ½ in (1.3 cm) from where they are all pulled back. This will make the head.

Tie

Pull over the end

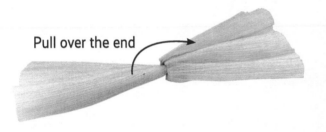

Step Three

To make arms, tear the last soaking husk in half to create a short piece. Roll that piece into a tube shape. Tie a piece of twine around each end.

Tie

Slide the arms between the layers of the husks that make up the body of the doll. Tie another piece of yarn under the arms to secure them and create a waist for your doll.

Optional: Use scrap fabric to make clothes for the doll.

Tie

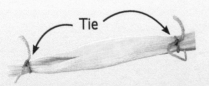

Glossary

alliances agreements by people, groups, or countries to work together

buffer something that acts as a protective barrier

cash crops plants grown to be sold for profit

colony a settlement made in a new area by a nation seeking to expand its territory

conquistadores leaders of Spanish efforts to explore and conquer the Americas

diplomatic relating to keeping good relations between people, groups, or countries

disgrace a source of shame or loss of honor

indentured servants people who work for someone for a set length of time to pay off debts

meetinghouses buildings for public gatherings to discuss town or colony business and sometimes for worship services

plantation a large farm that grows cash crops, such as tobacco, cotton, or sugar cane

profits money gained from selling a crop or product after all expenses have been paid

Quaker a member of the Religious Society of Friends, a Christian religious group

revolution a revolt against or overthrow of a government, leader, or system

shellfish crabs, clams, shrimp, lobsters, and other edible sea creatures that have shells but not backbones

stationery paper and materials used for writing

Read More

Casswell, Max. *My Life in the Plymouth Colony (My Place in History).* New York: Gareth Stevens Publishing (2018).

Jacobson, Bray. *The Thirteen Colonies (A Look at US History).* New York: Gareth Stevens Publishing (2018).

Omoth, Tyler. *Establishing the American Colonies (Foundations of Our Nation).* Lake Elmo, MN: Focus Readers (2018).

Learn More Online

1. Go to **www.factsurfer.com**

2. Enter "**Original Colonies**" into the search box.

3. Click on the cover of this book to see a list of websites.

Index

About the Author

Campbell Collison is the pseudonym for Cathy Collison and Janis Campbell. The two Michigan writers are both married and have two grown children each. They are avid history tourists and love uncovering fun facts, whether traveling to historic homes, presidential libraries, or national parks across the country. The friends have been writing partners for 25 years.